W9-BKD-898

Voices for Green Choices

# Ed Begley, Jr.

## Living Green

By Robert Grayson

Swampscott Public Library
61 Burrill Street
Swampscott, MA 01907

Crabtree Publishing Company
www.crabtreebooks.com

Crabtree Publishing Company

**Author:** Robert Grayson
**Publishing plan research and development:**
Sean Charlebois, Reagan Miller
Crabtree Publishing Company
**Editor:** Lynn Peppas
**Proofreader:** Crystal Sikkens
**Project coordinator:** Robert Walker
**Content and curriculum adviser:** Suzy Gazlay, M.A.
**Editorial:** Mark Sachner
**Photo research:** Ruth Owen
**Design:** Westgraphix/Tammy West
**Production coordinator:** Margaret Amy Salter
**Prepress technicians:** Margaret Amy Salter, Ken Wright
Written, developed, and produced by Water Buffalo Books

Cover photo: These bales of compacted cans represent one of the most energy-efficient developments in recent decades—the recycling of aluminum. Aluminum can be recycled indefinitely without losing any of its properties. In addition, recycling aluminum requires only about five percent of the energy needed to produce aluminum products from "scratch," making it the most cost-effective material to recycle. These factors, plus the reduction of so much trash that would otherwise be dumped into landfill sites, have made recycling aluminum one of Ed Begley, Jr.'s favorite methods of saving energy, conserving resources, and reducing clutter.

**Photo credits**:
Corbis: Chris Stewart, San Francisco Chronicle: page 9 (bottom); Bettmann: pages 12 (left), 18 (top), 26 (top and bottom); Hulton-Deutsch Collection: page 26 (center); Ted Soqui: page 39 (bottom)
Getty Images: David Livingston: front cover (inset), page 1; Charley Galley: page 4 (left); Michael Grecco: page 5 (bottom); Mat Szwajkos: page 6 (left); John M. Heller: page 10 (top); Gene Lester: page 13 (bottom); Allan Grant: page 14 (top); Alfred Eisenstaedt: page 16 (bottom); Matthew Simmons: page 30 (bottom); Frazer Harrison: page 32 (bottom); Amy Graves: page 37: (left); Chad Buchanan: pages 39 (top), 42 (bottom)
NASA: pages 16 (top), 29 (center)
Redferns: GAB Archives: page 25 (center)
REX: NBCUPHOTOBANK: pages 15 (bottom), 23 (bottom), 24 (bottom)
Shutterstock: pages 7, 8, 11 (bottom), 19 (left), 21 (top), 27, 28 (left), 29 (bottom), 30 (top and center), 33, 34, 35 (right), 36 (left), 38 (bottom), 40, 41, 42 (top)
Superstock: front cover (main)
Wikipedia: page 31 (top); Environmental Protection Agency (public domain image): page 20 (top)

**Library and Archives Canada Cataloguing in Publication**

Grayson, Robert, 1951-
Ed Begley, Jr. : living green / Robert Grayson.

(Voices for green choices)
Includes index.
ISBN 978-0-7787-4667-6 (bound).--ISBN 978-0-7787-4680-5 (pbk.)

1. Begley, Ed--Juvenile literature. 2. Green movement--Juvenile literature. 3. Sustainable living--Juvenile literature. 4. Environmentalists--United States--Biography--Juvenile literature. I. Title. II. Series: Voices for green choices

GE56.B43G73 2009 j640 C2009-900030-X

**Library of Congress Cataloging-in-Publication Data**

Grayson, Robert, 1951-
Ed Begley, Jr. : living green / by Robert Grayson.
p. cm. -- (Voices for green choices)
Includes index.
ISBN 978-0-7787-4680-5 (pbk. : alk. paper)
-- ISBN 978-0-7787-4667-6 (reinforced library binding : alk. paper)
1. Begley, Ed--Juvenile literature. 2. Environmentalists--United States--Biography--Juvenile literature. 3. Green movement--Juvenile literature. I. Title. II. Series.

GE56.B44G73 2009
640--dc22

2008054509

**Crabtree Publishing Company**
www.crabtreebooks.com 1-800-387-7650

Copyright © **2009 CRABTREE PUBLISHING COMPANY.** All rights reserved. No part of this publication may be reproduced, stored in a retrieval system or be transmitted in any form or by any means, electronic, mechanical, photocopying, recording, or otherwise, without the prior written permission of Crabtree Publishing Company.

**Published in Canada**
**Crabtree Publishing**
616 Welland Ave.
St. Catharines, Ontario
L2M 5V6

**Published in the United States**
**Crabtree Publishing**
PMB16A
350 Fifth Ave., Suite 3308
New York, NY 10118

**Published in the United Kingdom**
**Crabtree Publishing**
White Cross Mills
High Town, Lancaster
LA1 4XS

**Published in Australia**
**Crabtree Publishing**
386 Mt. Alexander Rd.
Ascot Vale (Melbourne)
VIC 3032

Contents

▲ Ed Begley, Jr. has used his fame to find new ways of helping the planet. He has also gotten other Hollywood stars interested in living green. Here he is shown at a massive tree-planting event in Los Angeles held to promote an eco-friendly Hollywood.

# Chapter 1

# Living Green Becomes Cool

What do Leonardo DiCaprio, Cameron Diaz, Jake Gyllenhaal, Edward Norton, George Clooney, Pierce Brosnan, Daryl Hannah, and Salma Hayek all have in common?

They all want to save the planet.

What's the big difference between them and Ed Begley, Jr.?

Ed Begley, Jr. has been living green for almost four decades, before it was cool to be actively working to preserve the environment. Even when people laughed at him for his unwavering commitment to preventing the planet from becoming a toxic wasteland, Ed's resolve remained strong.

## An Early Pioneer

His personal "crusade" to clean up the environment started long before Ed became a recognizable star, with countless movie and television roles to his credit. His big break came in the role of Dr. Victor Ehrlich on the hit NBC-TV series *St. Elsewhere* (1982–1988). It was a role for which he received six Emmy nominations. Even before *St. Elsewhere*, Ed was doing everything he could to save what he believed was our rather fragile planet Earth, the only home we have.

Ed was elated when so many Hollywood stars jumped on the green bandwagon, to lend their names to the campaign for a sustainable environment. Altogether, they brought attention to various ways to recycle, cut down on greenhouse gas emissions, and combat climate change. Although the title of the greenest man in Hollywood goes to Ed Begley, Jr., having all these stars on his side has made living green all the rage.

Just how committed has Ed been to environmental protection and preservation? He drove his electric car to the Academy Awards ceremonies back in 1991. When he arrived at the historic Shrine Auditorium in Los Angeles, Ed, all decked out in a tuxedo, had to look around for an electrical outlet to recharge the car—and he found one!

**"Greening" the Academy**

Sixteen years later, in 2007, the Academy of Motion Picture Arts and Sciences, sponsors of the Academy Awards, took up the "crusade."

◀ Ed Begley, Jr. has driven electric cars since 1970. One of his favorites was this Bradley GT II Electric, which he owned in the late 1980s.

▲ Celebrities have been embracing green living in droves. Here actress Cameron Diaz speaks at the July 7, 2007, Live Earth Concert for North America at Giants Stadium in East Rutherford, New Jersey.

The Academy announced that its annual awards presentation would be going green from then on, by incorporating "ecologically intelligent practices" into the events. That meant using everything from renewable wind power for the telecast to transporting staff and presenters to the site in hybrid cars. Not surprisingly, Ed Begley, Jr. is on the Board of Governors of the Academy (Actors Branch).

Hollywood stars who don't even know Ed have called him for advice on environmentally sustainable practices. Leonardo DiCaprio called him to ask if he and his father could come over to Ed's house and see his solar panels. Ed was more than happy to oblige. Lucy Liu called with solar power questions as well. Comedian Larry David called and wanted to know more about hybrid cars.

In the past few years, Ed and his family have earned a great deal of attention for their green lifestyle, though winning fame as environmentalists was never their goal. Ed's highly successful reality TV show, *Living with Ed*, has spawned a new generation of green-related docudramas, which portray actual families trying to maintain an eco-friendly lifestyle in the modern world. For Ed, his wife, actress Rachelle Carson, and their young daughter, Hayden, that simply meant turning on the cameras and letting them roll. *Living with Ed* debuted on cable's Home & Garden Television (HGTV) in January 2007 and was filmed at Ed's completely eco-friendly, two-bedroom house in the San Fernando Valley in California.

## Walking the Walk

The main focus of the program was the Begleys' totally green lifestyle and what it was like to live it—to both talk the talk and walk the walk. The show was filled with tips on how viewers could also live the green life and help save the environment. Some of the suggestions and ideas Ed talked about on the show were easy to put into practice; others were more difficult to carry out. Amazingly, Ed did all of them and showed viewers how they worked. He even demonstrated how living an environmentally sound life could save people money while saving the planet.

Ed's wife, Rachelle, provides a lot of comic relief on the show, as she challenges her husband's more far-out ideas. Rachelle can't help but complain about her husband's many Earth-saving projects for their home. "Ed's never concerned with how it looks," she pointed out.

She noted that when she left Ed home alone, it almost always meant running the risk of "coming home to some weird contraption," as her husband labored to find yet another way to save energy or recycle something.

Ed said the whole idea behind the show was to have fun with the concept of saving the planet and to have people become more aware of the environment. "We figured the best way

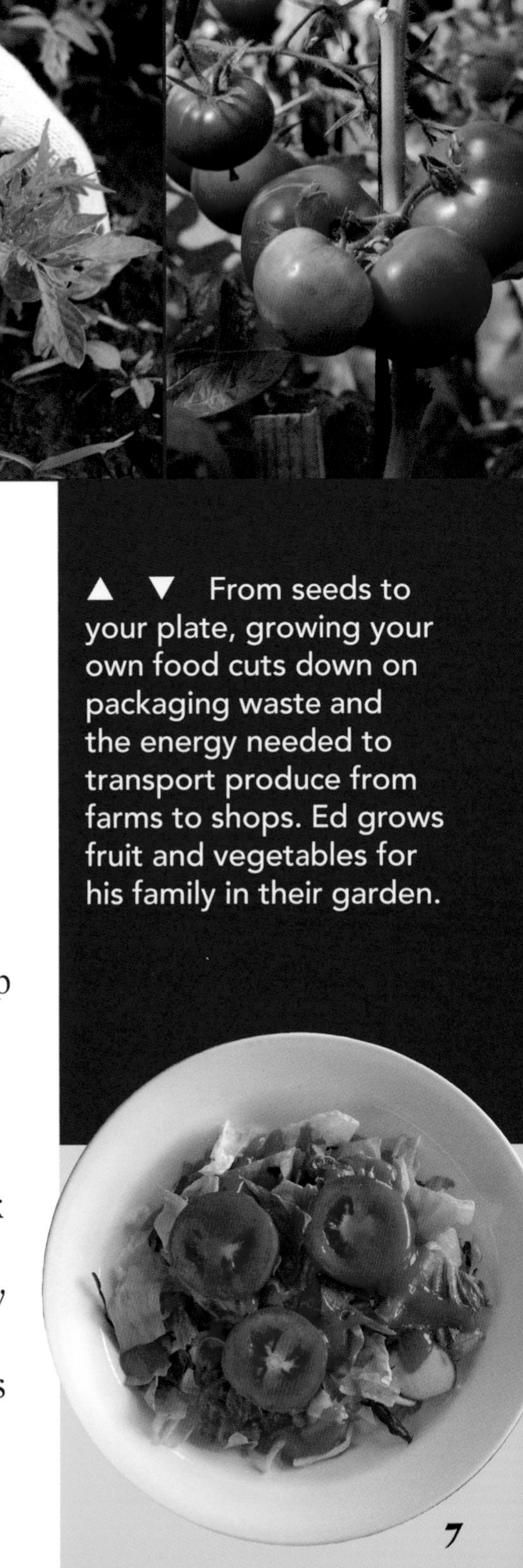

▲ ▼ From seeds to your plate, growing your own food cuts down on packaging waste and the energy needed to transport produce from farms to shops. Ed grows fruit and vegetables for his family in their garden.

**What Is a Carbon Footprint?**
Some people do not even realize they have a carbon footprint. In fact, everybody has a carbon footprint, and some are much bigger than others.

Carbon footprints are measured by the amount of energy we use going about our daily activities. Almost everything we do requires some form of energy, and in most cases fossil fuels are used to supply that energy. Fossil fuels emit carbon dioxide into the atmosphere, the main greenhouse gas causing climate change.

The less carbon dioxide produced by what we do, the smaller our carbon footprint and the less we contribute to destroying the environment. Ed Begley, Jr. is determined to make his carbon footprint as small as possible.

to get people's attention was with a reality-show format. We hoped people would find it amusing," he says. Nothing on the show is ever staged, no dialogue is ever written. It is all natural and as it happens, Ed notes: "We just have a very, very direct way of talking to each other."

While the show is being filmed Ed does what he usually does. He runs around the house unplugging, recycling, and gardening. This gets on his wife's nerves but they both agree that it's exactly how life is for them when the cameras are off.

Though some might think Ed takes being an environmentalist to extremes at times, viewers get a kick out of how Rachelle handles the situation on the show, as she struggles to get Ed to live green with a bit of style. Rachelle means what she says on the reality program, but she is also a committed environmentalist herself, sincerely

▶ Each of these activities requires the use of some kind of energy, and increases a person's carbon footprint.

concerned about shrinking her carbon footprint, the measure of how a person's activities affect the environment.

## Ed Gets Mail

From the very start, *Living with Ed* got noticed. People were watching the show and trying to do some of the things they saw on it. Ed started getting e-mails from all over the country. People were writing to Ed, asking him questions and seeking his advice on living green, and he was more than happy to respond. At times, when various episodes of *Living with Ed* ran for the first time, Ed would get more than 100 e-mails a day from both eco-conscious fans and Earth-saving novices.

Ed even has his own Web site (www.edbegley.com), where he has information about his acting career and his environmental efforts. The Web site has been live since 2005, but when the reality show debuted in 2007, it sparked much more e-mail to Ed's site than in the past. He says 40 percent of his e-mails are

◀ Solar-powered ovens use heat from the Sun's rays to cook food. Ed likes to cook soup, rice, and beans on the outdoor oven, which can heat up to 375 degrees Fahrenheit (199 degrees Celsius) on a sunny day.

▲ Ed followed up his successful television series, *Living with Ed*, with a book based in part on the show. Published in 2008, *Living Like Ed* gives reasonably priced tips on bringing a green lifestyle into the home. It also provides interesting facts about the benefits of living green.

from a more conservative crowd of people who write, "I don't always agree with you politically, but I like your show and where do I get a solar oven?"

The success of *Living with Ed* has proved to its star that "People are ready to make changes, if we can get the word out that there's really no sacrifice involved, that you can do a lot of these things, and it really won't cost you in any meaningful way. That is to say we still can get people a cool beverage and a warm shower. We're just going to do it more efficiently. People are really on board."

During the second season of *Living with Ed*, Ed and Rachelle visited the homes of other stars to see what they were doing to live green. That provided some interesting insights, including a look at singer Jackson Browne's ranch, which is completely off the power grid. The home is powered by a wind turbine and solar power, has wood-burning stoves for heat, and it is built from masonry to stay cool without air-conditioning even on the hottest days.

## Going Green Catching On

In 2008, all the episodes of *Living with Ed* from the first two seasons were re-aired on Green Planet TV, and some of the episodes are available on DVD. Ed has also written a book, *Living Like Ed*, that was based on his television show. The book was published in 2008 and is a complete guide to the eco-friendly life. Ed shows readers how to live life in an environmentally sound way. Other environmental experts offer some commentary in the book, as does Ed's wife, who often has a semi-humorous take on the topics. The book is much more than a how-to guide. Ed gives reasons why things should be done, such as recycling and using energy-saving light bulbs, and what the result of energy-saving projects will be. He also offers less costly alternatives to some of the more pricey green-living practices.

While Ed traces his first real taste of environmentalism back to 1969, when he was almost 20 years old. Caring about nature and conservation was something that was actually deeply rooted in his upbringing, and was just waiting to break out.

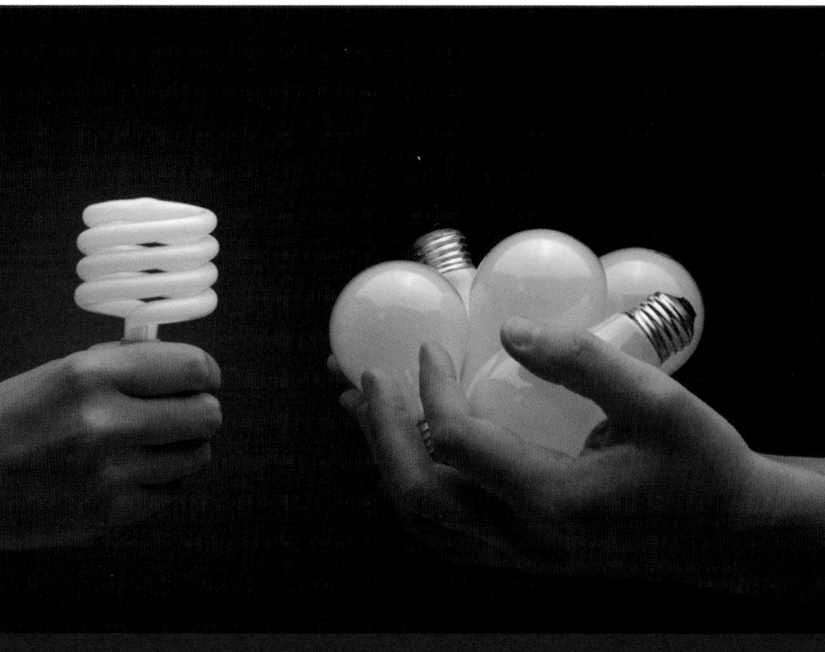

▲ A Compact Fluorescent Light, or CFL (left), using 18 watts of power can give out light that equals the 60 watts of power emitted by incandescent light bulbs (right). Ed says that some of the CFLs he has in his home have lasted 15 years!

**The Light Goes Off**

How many environmentalists does it take to convince folks to change a light bulb? Or, better yet, to change all their light bulbs?

Changing from incandescent light bulbs in homes and small offices is easy, and it's a great way to embark on an environmentally sustainable lifestyle. Those funny-looking, squiggly light bulbs sitting on store shelves are known as Compact Fluorescent Lights (CFLs).

CFLs use between 50 and 80 percent less energy than the incandescent light bulbs that most people use. CFLs can last up to ten times longer than those old energy-eating light bulbs. CFLs may cost more than incandescent light bulbs, but they more than make up for the initial cost by lasting longer and saving on overall energy bills. Just think about it: Electric lights account for as much as 25 percent of a home's total energy bill!

Nearly anywhere traditional light bulbs are used, a CFL can be inserted instead. CFLs come in a variety of sizes, shapes, and styles, including three-way.

Even changing just one light bulb from incandescent to CFL can have a positive impact on the environment and the electric bill.

Changing to CFLs helps save energy, but doesn't get the whole job done by itself. People still have to remember that the last one to leave a room turns off the light.

Chapter 2

# Born to Act

As a very small child, Ed Begley, Jr. was taught the concept of conservation, even though those lessons had nothing to do with the environment directly.

Ed's dad grew up during the Great Depression in the 1930s, the worst economic collapse in the history of the United States. He taught Ed not to waste or use things he didn't need, to repair and reuse things whenever possible, and to live modestly. Ed still uses these lessons today to help shrink his carbon footprint.

Edward James Begley, Jr. was born on September 16, 1949, in Los Angeles, California. He was the second child of well-known character actor Ed Begley, Sr. and actress Allene Jeanne Sanders. He has an older sister, Allene Johanna Begley, born in 1948. By the time Ed, Jr. was two years old, the family had moved from California to Merrick, Long Island, New York, where they lived until 1962.

▲ Much of what Ed teaches about reusing things rather than discarding them has roots in what these women from the 1930s are doing—making a quilt from swatches of leftover fabric. Their activity was born out of the economic hard times of the Great Depression.

## Ed's Dad: Onstage and Onscreen

Ed Begley, Sr. was born in Hartford, Connecticut. He was a radio actor as a teenager, worked on the Broadway stage in more than a dozen plays, acted in about 40 movies, and appeared in more than 250 television shows. He did not have to convince his son to go into acting. It was something Ed, Jr. wanted to do ever since he was three years old.

Even though Ed's father was a well-respected and recognizable character actor, Ed lived a fairly normal suburban life, attending a Catholic school on Long Island and even working as a paperboy. He frequently went to the movies with his friends, and his father encouraged him to join the Cub Scouts and later the Boy Scouts, where Ed learned to love and appreciate the outdoors and all it had to offer.

Besides camping out or watching movies, Ed happily recalled that, as a young boy, he made several trips with his father when he was performing in plays in Boston and Philadelphia. Ed vividly remembers being backstage and sitting in theater dressing rooms as actors counted down the final seconds before the curtain went up. The trips with his father only confirmed what Ed already knew: "The energy of the theater was unmistakable."

◀ Actress Rita Moreno gives Ed Begley, Sr. a big kiss backstage after he won the 1962 Best Supporting Actor Academy Award for his role in the film *Sweet Bird of Youth*. Ed, Jr. still proudly displays the award in his home today.

**Smog, L.A.-Style**
In October 1954, smog in Los Angeles was so pervasive that it forced schools and industries to shut down for the month. Some people felt they needed to put on gas masks to go outdoors safely (right).

The smog gradually became worse as the decade continued, and heavy smog became commonplace in Los Angeles in the 1960s. When the environmental movement grew stronger after the first Earth Day in 1970, Los Angeles smog was the target of many environmental activists, who forced political leaders to draft strict clean-air regulations to address the problem. Today, Los Angeles is winning its battle against smog.

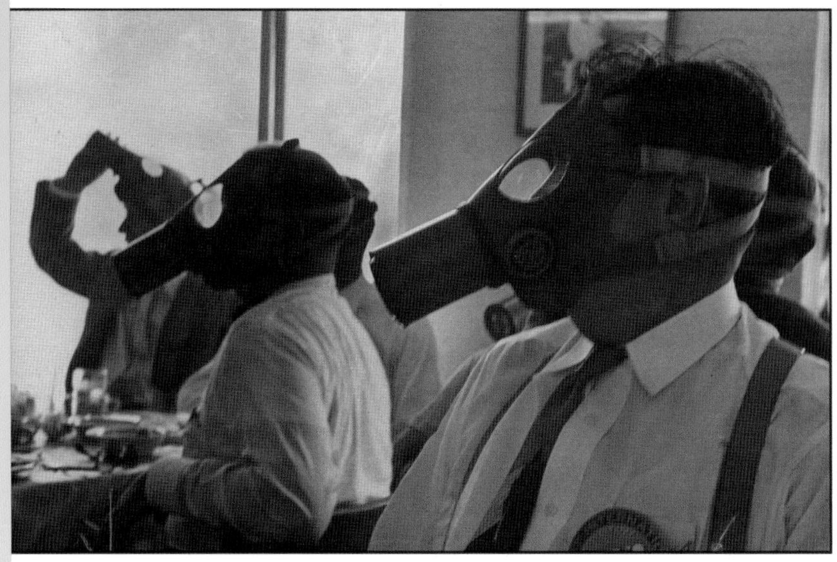

## Back to California

After Ed Begley, Sr. won an Oscar in 1962 for Best Supporting Actor in *Sweet Bird of Youth*, the family moved back west to Van Nuys, California, where Ed, Sr. was getting a lot of roles on television shows. Meanwhile Ed, Jr., who had become an avid Boy Scout, began to notice the poor air quality in Van Nuys. He couldn't run down the block without wheezing, and smog made it impossible to see the mountains surrounding the area where he lived.

Ed hoped he would get his break in show business when he was around ten years old. Although Ed's dad wanted him to get roles on his own, he did help his young son get some auditions. Still, Ed had trouble getting work. Eventually, he realized that he kept coming up short because he "hadn't trained as an actor." Ed said that as a youngster he just felt that if his dad could act, he could too. Once he realized that wasn't true, he took some classes, and in 1967, while he was still in his teens, Ed landed a small part on the primetime situation comedy *My Three Sons*, starring Fred MacMurray. The part took just one day to film, but Ed was happy for the breakthrough.

As it turned out, 1967 was a big year for Ed. That spring, he graduated from Van Nuys High School, where his favorite subject was science. His passion for science would serve him well later in life as he advocated for environmentally sustainable living. Besides Ed, Van Nuys High School has had some other famous alumni through the years, including Marilyn Monroe, Robert Redford, Paula Abdul, Natalie Wood, and many others.

## A Start in Comedy

In the fall of 1967, Ed enrolled at Los Angeles Valley College, majoring in theater and cinematography, or movie making. In college he met a fellow who liked to walk into classes backwards, trip over desks in the classroom, and bang into doors. His classmate was the yet-to-be-discovered comic, Michael Richards, who later became famous playing Jerry Seinfeld's zany neighbor Kramer on the hit TV comedy, *Seinfeld*.

◀ Jerry Seinfeld, left, with Michael Richards, who played Kramer on the hit TV comedy series *Seinfeld*. For a short time, Michael Richards was Ed's standup comedy partner.

### Taking Comedy Seriously

Ed Begley, Jr. always knew he had a good sense of humor, but he also knew that it took more than that to be a great comic, so he spent a lot of time studying the comic greats of the past.

Ed believes something can be learned from every great comic. He points out that some comics specialize in physical comedy, while others use no props; some become characters, and some just write great material. Some work best alone, others work well only in teams. He has studied Charlie Chaplin, Laurel and Hardy, Jonathan Winters, Lily Tomlin, Richard Pryor, Jerry Seinfeld, and other great comics who came before him to learn the art of comedy.

Ed took a critical look at these comics' material, their timing, and their interaction with the audience, and Ed's comic training helped him when performing comedic roles in movies and on TV. Then, to polish his skills, Ed found that there was no better way than to go out, get up in front of the crowd, and perform.

Richards and Ed formed a comedy team for a short time in 1968 and did improvisational work at comedy clubs around Los Angeles. Meanwhile, Ed was also going after cinematography work and labored as both a comic and a cameraman, making documentaries and TV commercials. Begley and Richards had some success, but their act was inconsistent. Some days they would make the audience laugh; other days the act fell flat.

After a short time together, Richards left the act, and Ed decided to try his hand at solo standup comedy. First he worked in local Los Angeles clubs, and then he went on the road. He was good enough to play big arenas and open for singers such as John Sebastian and Loggins and Messina. Ed wrote his own material and was getting good reviews, but he never lost interest in acting or the environment.

## Eye-Opening Experiences

Several things happened that brought Ed's focus back to doing something to help the planet. On June 22, 1969, Ed was shocked to see on the news that the Cuyahoga River in Cleveland, Ohio had

▶ Ed Begley, Jr. remembers when the Cuyahoga River in Cleveland, Ohio caught fire in 1969. Here three men in a motorboat take a sample of the water from the river, which is visibly polluted.

▲ Photos of "Earthrise," such as this one sent back to Earth from the *Apollo 11* Moon mission in July 1969, inspired Ed Begley, Jr. to take action to help the planet.

*"I became aware of the fragility of this planet when viewing the Earth rise pictures taken from the moon. It had a profound effect upon me because I saw that, for better or worse, we have nowhere else to go. Although the problems seem immense and no one individual is going to fix everything, there is a lot we can do as individuals."*

- Ed Begley, Jr., describing his response to the first Moon landing in 1969 on his Web site (www.edbegley.com)

caught fire. "It was such a stunning thought, a river so polluted it would burn," he recalled.

Then, on July 20, 1969, Ed was glued to his TV, as were so many Americans, watching the first astronauts step foot on the Moon. He saw pictures of Earth that the astronauts from *Apollo 11* were sending from their vantage point in outer space.

These events, coupled with the choking smog hanging over Los Angeles, prompted Ed to take action when the first Earth Day observance took place on April 22, 1970. He started recycling and composting and purchased his first electric car, which he laughs about now. It was basically a golf

▲ During the first Earth Day—April 22, 1970—junior high school students demonstrate in Kirkwood, Missouri, a suburb of St. Louis. They are protesting air pollution caused by automobile emissions. The students also participated in Earth Day lectures, workshops, panel discussions, and debates about environmental issues, including pollution and population control.

cart with a horn, a windshield, and windshield wipers. It didn't go more than 15 miles per hour (24 km/h). It also could go for only 15 miles (24 km) on each charge and then would conk out. Ed was determined to do what he could to curb pollution, so he drove the car despite its drawbacks. Friends still kid him about that car, calling him a pioneer of electric cars, not because he invented them, but because he was one of the first to drive them.

### Just Do It

At first, Ed didn't talk much about what he was doing or going to do to the save the environment. He just did it. Since he started living green in 1970, Ed's commitment to the environment has never waned, and his efforts have grown.

Just a few days after Earth Day in 1970, Ed was shocked by the news that his dad had died suddenly of a heart attack in Hollywood. He was 69 years old. "I miss him every day," Ed said. Ed Begley, Sr.'s Academy Award is prominently displayed in his son's home. Ed's dad never got a chance to see his son's great success as an actor, but Ed says he knows his dad was proud of him. Since his father's death, Ed has dedicated all his efforts on behalf of the environment in memory of Ed Begley, Sr. Ed Begley, Jr. was more determined than ever to follow in his father's footsteps and become a successful actor.

# Chapter 3

# Branching Out

▲ In 1970, Ed's efforts to become a full-fledged vegetarian were thwarted because vegetarian-style cuisine was simply not offered in many places at that time. With increased concern about the environment, animal rights, and health, vegetarianism became popular in the late twentieth century. Today, many restaurants cater to vegetarians.

During the late 1960s and early 1970s, Ed Begley, Jr. was working as a cameraman by day and doing his standup comedy routine at nights and on weekends. He still pursued acting jobs and had some success in landing small parts on popular network television shows of the time, including the crime dramas *Mannix*, *The F.B.I.*, and *Owen Marshall: Counselor at Law*. He also worked in a comedy here and there, such as *Love, American Style* and *Happy Days*, and in a few movies. In 1972, he landed a role on an episode of the hit TV series *M*A*S*H*, but Ed was not able to get enough acting work to rise above struggling-actor status.

## A Vegetarian Lifestyle

Regardless of how things were going for him in Hollywood, Ed continued his environmental efforts. He found it more difficult to maintain his vegetarian lifestyle, which he had adopted on Earth Day in 1970, and altered his eating habits about a year after turning vegetarian. "I started eating some fish because I couldn't find vegetarian food when I traveled. I'd do a movie in some distant city…and they wouldn't have anything to eat," Ed recalled. He never went back to eating red meat and returned to being a full-fledged vegetarian in 1992.

**Green with Envy**

Even when living an eco-friendly lifestyle, people try to outdo each other.

In 1970, when Ed Begley, Jr. purchased his first alternative mode of transportation, an electric car, it cost him $950—and it wasn't a pretty car. But it got him where he wanted to go, and it didn't pollute the air. Ed's commitment to clean air was so strong that he drove the car, even though the glances he was getting had nothing to do with the car being incredibly cool.

Times have changed, and now stars are lining up to drive a set of wheels powered by alternative fuels.

◀ When Ed Begley, Jr. first drove an electric car in 1970, it was nothing more than a golf cart with a windshield. The 1973 General Motors Urban Electric Car (left) was a small step up from Ed's first set of electric wheels.

It appeared as though things were going to change for Ed in 1973 when Larry Gelbart, one of the writers for *M*A*S*H*, created a new series, called *Roll Out*, which also dealt with the military. It took several seasons for *M*A*S*H* to find an audience, but TV executives were not as patient with *Roll Out*, and the show was canceled after only five episodes. Ed went back to taking character roles on TV and landing small but growing movie parts.

## Some Steady Work

Ed got a recurring role on the hit sitcom *Mary Hartman, Mary Hartman* in 1976. A parody of TV soap operas, the program was considered a breakthrough show at the time because it tackled

▲ This car of the future, a Honda FCSport, is powered by a hydrogen fuel cell. A big hit at the Los Angeles Auto Show in November 2008, the car already has people lining up to buy it.

some controversial subjects.

His personal life was also becoming more settled, and Ed married his girlfriend, Ingrid Taylor, in October of 1976. Ingrid worked in movies, too—not as an actor, but in special effects. The couple had two children: a daughter, Amanda, in October 1977, and a son, Nicholas, in January 1979.

Ed was now getting bigger roles in movies and recurring roles on TV. Many fans remember him as Ensign Greenbean—later Flight Sergeant Greenbean—on the popular TV version of the franchise sci-fi thriller *Battlestar Galactica* from 1978 to 1979. Through the years, the program has become a cult favorite of science-fiction fans.

**Hydrogen Power**

One group of must-have cars are hydrogen powered, and they can go as far as 270 miles (435 km) on a tank of fuel. These cars have a few drawbacks, such as the fact that they have to be refueled by a trained professional who knows how to handle liquid hydrogen, but they emit nothing but water.

Who could doubt a star's commitment to the environment if he or she were seen driving one of these hydrogen-powered mean machines? The cars probably won't be on the market for a while, but a few prototypes are out there, and automakers hope to get even more mileage out of them by having movie stars tooling around in them as a way to build demand for the cars before they are mass-produced.

## A Favorite Part

The blond-haired actor played what turned out to be one of his most enjoyable roles ever in 1979, when he appeared in the original version of the hit comedy movie *The In-Laws* with Peter Falk and Alan Arkin. Ed says the movie's set was full of madcap antics, with something funny always happening both on and off camera.

Though Ed was getting more roles now, he wasn't getting where he wanted to go in the business. He wanted steadier work, such as a full-time role on a TV show, which was something more than he was being offered. He wanted a better choice of roles, parts with greater depth and character development. By 1982, for the first time in the 15 years he had been acting, Ed was thinking about leaving Hollywood and giving up acting.

He had talked to his wife, Ingrid, about moving to Atlanta. Ed had been in Atlanta when he was touring with his stand-up comedy routine, and he liked the city. He had some friends in Atlanta and was seriously considering moving there and trying something new, such as maybe getting a local TV or radio talk show. He wasn't exactly sure what he was going to do, other than move out of Hollywood and see what happened.

## A Pivotal Role

Just weeks away from moving to Atlanta, Ed got a call about a part in a new television show called *St. Elsewhere*. It was the part of Dr. Peter White. Though still determined to move in a new direction, Ed decided to show up for this one last audition. The show was being produced by MTM

Enterprises, the production company behind the critically acclaimed police drama *Hill Street Blues* of the same era. Like *Hill Street Blues*, *St. Elsewhere* featured an ensemble cast, but this show would be a medical drama.

The show dealt with serious medical issues, and matters of life and death. It also incorporated dark comedy, and things generally left unspoken on network television. Even the name of the show poked fun at a medical taboo, because "St. Elsewhere" is slang in the medical profession for a hospital that mostly treats poor, uninsured patients whom no other hospital wants to help. The whole concept piqued Ed's interest, but he didn't get the role of Dr. Peter White. Actor Terence Knox did.

The show's producers liked Ed's work. That's why they had called him to try out for the role of Dr. White in the first place. They came up with a minor character for him to play in the show—Dr. Victor Ehrlich.

◀ Ed Begley, Jr. (Dr. Victor Ehrlich), left, talks to Howie Mandel (Dr. Wayne Fiscus) in a scene from an episode of *St. Elsewhere*. Both Ed and Howie appeared in the entire six-season run of the show.

Ed found that people related to the plight of the doctors, staff, and patients at St. Eligius, a fictional run-down teaching hospital with no money, located in South Boston. Ed received six Emmy nominations for his work on the show—one for every year the show was produced. The Emmy is television's highest honor. He was also nominated for a Golden Globe Award for Best Supporting Actor in a Series in 1987 for his role in *St. Elsewhere*. Ironically, the role of Dr. Peter White, which Ed originally tried out for, was eliminated from the show in the 1985 season.

## A Groundbreaker

A groundbreaking series, *St. Elsewhere* got Ed noticed. Other members of the cast were noticed as well. The show is credited with launching the career of Denzel Washington, who played Dr. Phillip

▶ The cast of *St. Elsewhere* was considered an ensemble, but many famous stars emerged from that show. Among the cast were the following actors (clockwise from lower left): Academy Award-winner Denzel Washington (Dr. Phillip Chandler), Ed Begley, Jr. (Dr. Victor Ehrich), David Morse (Dr. Jack Morrison), Howie Mandel (Dr. Wayne Fiscus), Mark Harmon (Dr. Robert Caldwell), Sagan Lewis (Dr. Jaqueline Wade), and Stephen Furst (Dr. Elliot Axelrod).

Chandler. *TV Guide* once called the show the best dramatic series of all time. Unlike other medical shows in the 1960s and 1970s, the doctors portrayed in *St. Elsewhere* were not flawless or always likable. They weren't always right. Some patients on the show didn't like their doctors; some doctors didn't like their patients. The show dealt with topics that had never been discussed on a TV show before, such as AIDS, Alzheimer's disease, and the state of health care for the poor.

Doctors on *St. Elsewhere* were not always successful in saving patients' lives, and many stories had sad endings, as in real-life medical cases. Some patients were left to live with worsening medical conditions and others were told there was no hope. Not every doctor on the show was top-notch, and some of the doctors had their own pressing personal problems that distracted them from the care of their patients.

▲ One of Ed's most enjoyable roles was playing "Stumpy" Pepys in the 1984 Rob Reiner movie *This Is Spinal Tap.*

**Hard Rockin' Ed**

During his tenure on *St. Elsewhere*, Ed stayed put in California and also made movies, including the Rob Reiner film *This Is Spinal Tap* in 1984. The movie was made like a documentary, but it is about a completely fictitious rock band, called Spinal Tap, that was supposed to have been popular in the 1970s and then hit bottom in the 1980s. The film pokes fun at bands like Led Zeppelin and other hard rockers of the 1970s.

Ed plays one of the band's early drummers, John "Stumpy" Pepys. Like bands of that era, Spinal Tap goes through breakups, arguments, and mysterious deaths. Ed's character dies in a bizarre gardening accident, but no details of that mishap are ever given in the film. Ed enjoyed doing the film because it was quirky and oddly humorous. The film was such an authentic takeoff of the bands of the 1970s that some people thought Spinal Tap had actually existed.

**Energy from Sunshine—An Early View**
Centuries ago, people would use magnifying glasses to direct the Sun's rays onto wood. When the wood caught fire, it could then be used for heating or cooking. This was the first known use of solar energy.

In the 1860s, French scientist Augustin Mouchot invented a steam engine completely powered by the Sun, and brought solar power into the industrial age. He continued to work over the next 20 years to upgrade his invention. Charles Greeley Abbott, a United States astrophysicist, invented a solar boiler in 1936, and this device was considered a major step forward in the harnessing of solar energy.

*St. Elsewhere* strayed from the TV show formula of the time, which had everybody living happily ever after at the end of each episode, no matter what happened to them during the show. Every medical TV series since *St. Elsewhere*, including *ER*, has taken something from the highly acclaimed show and used it to their benefit, including incorporating the latest diseases in storylines, even if there is no cure for them.

▶ Inventors in the 1800s devised a solar-powered printing press. It is shown above being tested in August 1882 in Paris. An early effort at solar-powered transportation, this 1912 Baker Electric Model (right) received its energy from the solar panel mounted on the car's roof. Dr. Maria Telkes, shown (below right) in the 1950s, was one of the world's premier inventors in the field of solar energy. Here she discusses one of her creations, a solar oven that resembles the one Ed Begley, Jr. uses outside his home.

◀ Contemporary applications of solar power include (shown clockwise from upper left) a solar power plant and a solar-powered office building, parking meter, traffic light, and house.

**Energy from Sunshine—A More Recent View**

Solar water heaters became popular around World War II and were used in homes until the mid-1950s, when low-cost natural gas became the leading home heating fuel in the United States.

Oil shortages in the 1970s prompted people to begin looking at solar energy again, and today it is used to heat homes and office buildings, to generate electricity, and to run water heaters. Energy generated by the Sun is completely clean and renewable. Even though solar energy is being used more today than in the past, researchers are continuing to search for ways to make it more efficient, accessible, and less expensive.

## Getting Ready to Go Green

The success of *St. Elsewhere*, and some of the movies Ed was making after he got the role of Dr. Ehrlich on that hit show, gave him the chance to pursue his ultimate goal of getting off the power grid. He could afford to install some of the latest environment-saving technologies in his home, such as a solar hot water system.

Ed was doing everything he could in his life to shrink what today would be called his carbon footprint, and he felt good about that.

Chapter 4

# Earth's Best Friend

In the 1980s, Hollywood was not even close to going green, so it is not surprising that hardly anyone shared Ed's passion for such issues as solar energy or battling smog.

Back then, some in Hollywood thought Ed was a bit of a fanatic when it came to environmental causes, but Ed said that never bothered him and he never tried to push his views on others. Ed was convinced that what he was doing to save the planet simply made sense.

In September 1987, environmentalists got a big boost with the signing of the Montreal Protocol. Twenty-four nations got together and signed the international treaty to start eliminating the production of substances that are believed to be depleting Earth's protective ozone layer. The treaty went into effect on January 1, 1989. Ed thought the treaty meant the environmental movement was going to gain some much-needed momentum, and he was right.

Meanwhile, *St. Elsewhere* was giving Ed the chance to truly showcase his range of talent. His role on the hit show led to offers of bigger and better movie roles on the big screen. It also gave Ed freedom of choice. He was now able to act in the best scripts that came his way, rather than having to do every part he was offered, whether he liked the work or not.

▲ A choking haze of smog blankets Los Angeles. It was scenes like this that convinced Ed Begley, Jr. in the late 1960s that something had to be done about air pollution.

## Going for the "Best Material"

"Always go for the best material if you have that choice," Ed is fond of saying. During his career, he saw that the best material always attracted the best cast, the best directors, and the best camera people. It usually already had the best writers who wrote the best parts.

Once Ed felt what it was like to choose the parts he really wanted, he never wanted to give up that freedom. He vowed not to go the route of many actors he knew who turned down a good script, dealing with a solid subject, in favor of a bad script with a role that paid more money. Ed chose a different road instead, following his father's philosophy of

◀ A view of the ozone hole over Antarctica, taken from space in 2006, when scientists reported that the ozone layer was becoming severely depleted.

**The Montreal Protocol**

In effect since 1989, the Montreal Protocol is considered the greatest international environmental treaty ever drafted. Even though just 24 nations, including the United States and Canada, signed on at first, now more than 190 nations have signed the protocol.

The agreement phases out the use and production of ozone-depleting chemicals (ODCs), such as chlorofluorocarbons (CFCs), which are used in air-conditioners and some cleaning processes. The ozone layer protects Earth and all life on it from harsh, damaging rays from the Sun. Among other things, these rays can cause skin cancer. So far, the treaty has been successful in phasing out the use or production of 95 percent of ODCs.

The impact has been very positive, with signs that the ozone layer seems to be slowly recovering and could actually go back to its original state if the rescue work continues.

◀ CFC propellants in aerosol cans have been banned because CFCs damage Earth's ozone layer.

living a modest lifestyle. That meant keeping life simple, which also fit in with Ed's environmental vision.

Not everything was going as Ed had hoped. In October 1989, a short time after *St. Elsewhere* completed its run, Ed and his wife Ingrid divorced. It was not something Ed was happy about, but he kept in close contact with his two children from that marriage, and he still does to this day. His son, Nicholas, is now an electrical engineer, and his daughter, Amanda, works with her dad on one of his environmental projects.

### Greening His New Home

To keep busy outside of work, Ed bought a small, two-bedroom home in the San Fernando Valley in 1990. Ed loved the house, which was built in 1936. There was nothing energy-efficient about it, so Ed's work was cut out for him as he aimed to make the home totally green and, if possible, off the power

▲ Solar water heaters such as this one (above) provide hot water in a cost-effective way. Both solar water heaters and solar-powered garden lights (below), use free sunshine as a source of energy.

▶ At a press conference in June 2005 in Los Angeles, Ed speaks in support of a proposal to give financial rewards to builders of affordable housing who increase the number of solar-powered units installed in low-income homes.

▶ An electric bike with a battery-powered, lightweight electric engine makes this mode of transportation a great alternative to cars for running daily errands.

grid. He was ready, willing, and committed to achieving his goal.

Though Ed likes to joke that his rather normal-looking home is considered a shack by Hollywood standards, that's just fine as far as he is concerned. The 1,700-square-foot (160-square-meter) home that Ed bought is the same size as the home he lived in as a child, and that's big enough for him. In between working on movie projects and TV shows, Ed worked on his house. Some of the projects he did himself, since he has had a knack for carpentry ever since he was a youngster.

Though Ed made some big energy-saving changes soon after he moved into the home, such as installing solar panels, he continues to make environmentally sound improvements. And don't think that a completely green house can't have all the amenities that many Americans want, such as a white picket fence. Ed has one right outside his home—only it is made entirely from recycled plastic milk jugs!

**Ready, Set...Pedal!**

Anyone who has seen or read anything about Ed Begley, Jr. knows that he is a big fan of the bicycle. Like walking, bicycling keeps a car and all its pollutants off the road, and it is wonderful exercise for the rider. In areas with heavy traffic, it also helps get around all the congestion.

Ed even uses an electric bike that is a "hybrid" of sorts in the bicycle world. Unlike the hybrid car, however, which runs partly on an electric engine and partly on a gasoline engine, a hybrid bike is powered partly by human pedaling and partly by a battery-powered electric engine.

Electric bikes are a perfect alternative to cars, especially in urban areas. They have hardly any impact on the environment, so they are great for people who want to reduce their carbon footprint. As a plus, it costs much less to operate an electric bike than a car.

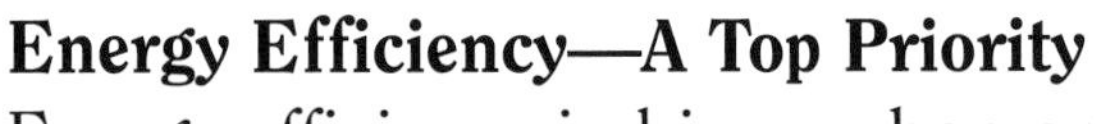

## Energy Efficiency—A Top Priority

Energy efficiency in his new home was Ed's first concern. He insulated the home properly and installed an energy-saving thermostat and double-pane windows. He believes these things are great first steps that everyone can take, even if they can't or don't want to make the move to solar panels right away. Does having an environmentally sound home mean sacrificing modern conveniences such as air-conditioning? Absolutely not, Ed maintains. He put solar-powered air-conditioning in his home shortly after he got the house, and the air-conditioning is still running at peak efficiency. Ed's home is superinsulated, so he doesn't have to run the cooling system very much.

One of the things Ed looked for when searching for a new home was proximity to stores and restaurants so he could walk or ride a bicycle to do daily errands. Outside his home, Ed was becoming known for riding his bicycle to movie previews and big Hollywood events. If the event was too far away to cycle, there was always mass transit. Even in the 1990s Ed was still driving the latest version of the electric car, which stood out from all those limousines and sports cars lined up outside big, fancy Hollywood-style events.

Ed was also attending events—environmental events—not as a star, but as a concerned member of the world population. It was at one of these events in 1993 that he met his future wife, actress Rachelle Carson. Rachelle was an environmental activist even

▼ Ed Begley, Jr. arrives at the first "green" Oscars in 2007 with his wife, Rachelle Carson. Ed is a member of the Board of Governors of the Academy of Motion Picture Arts and Sciences.

before she met Ed. In fact, she was named after an environmental visionary, the late biologist Rachel Carson. Rachel Carson wrote the book *Silent Spring* in 1962. In it, she warned the world about the uncontrolled use of pesticides and their impact on the environment. There was no need for Ed to convert Rachelle to the ranks of planet saver. She was already with the program.

### Saving Money While Saving the Planet

While Ed was single and dating Rachelle, he was making tremendous progress in his quest to be off the power grid. Naturally, a single person uses less energy than a family, but even at that Ed was able to cut his power bill to an astounding $100 a year. That's one point Ed likes to make—that all the steps he was taking to save the planet actually turned out to be saving him money as well. Though Ed found

▲◄ A rug made from recycled fabric scraps (above) and shopping bags (left) made from recycled paper help save the planet's natural resources.

**Recycling, Reusing, and Renewing**

Products made from paper, glass, plastic, clothes, aluminum, metal, and countless other things can be recycled. From an environmental standpoint, the best thing about recycling is that it always takes less energy to make something from recycled materials than from new materials. Cutting back on the use of energy also helps cut back on greenhouse gas emissions that contribute to global warming. Recycling anything almost always guarantees having a positive impact on the environment.

Environmental activists like Ed Begley, Jr. believe almost everything can be recycled or simply reused. An animal shelter may be able to use someone's old towels, drapes, or throw rugs. A thrift shop may be able to repair and reuse old toys.

In addition to reducing much of the pollution that is created in the manufacturing of new products, recycling and reusing are things everybody can do. They also give people a chance to be creative and think of ways that others can use something they don't need anymore.

that what he was doing to shrink his carbon footprint took some work, he was buying less, reusing more, taking up less space, and honing his philosophy of living more simply, so others could simply live better. Ed didn't want to infringe on anyone else's space.

Sometimes Ed had to interrupt his environmental projects to get some acting done. He was as busy as ever in the 1990s. One of his TV projects coincided with his environmental work. He hosted an educational TV show, called *Earth Aid* (1990–1991), which explored environmental topics. Several of those shows have since been released on DVD. His voice could be heard in the popular animated *Batman* TV series in 1992, and he appeared in many TV shows, including a *Columbo* episode in 1994. Ed also had roles in more movies in the 1990s, including an uncredited one in the 1995 blockbuster, *Batman Forever*.

## Influential Friends

Ed was also making some important friends in the environmental community including Vice President Al Gore and Robert F. Kennedy, Jr., an environmental attorney and son of the late United States Senator Robert F. Kennedy. Kennedy has talked on many occasions about how much he respects Ed for his long-term commitment to keep the planet environmentally sustainable. Kennedy has also said that Ed has a much greater sense of social responsibility than most people do.

As a testament to Ed's commitment to the environment, he has been asked to serve on the board of many environmental groups, and he has

**How Can You Reduce Your Footprint?**
People can join Ed in reducing their carbon footprint by doing even simple things. Shrinking a carbon footprint is a conscious decision. As Ed said, it's about making choices that will help save the planet.

If driving someplace is necessary, perhaps several people going to the same place could carpool, or take a train or a bus (above). Turn off lights, and the TV, too, when no one is in a room. Use energy-efficient light bulbs and electric products. Turn down the thermostat (below) during the day if nobody is home.

happily agreed. Ed is interested in more than simply lending his name to these organizations. He wants to be an active board member and has even chaired some of them. When these organizations meet, Ed is usually on hand.

One of those organizations is the Environmental Media Association (EMA), which Ed chaired at one time. The EMA has helped the film industry change its wasteful habits. With guidance from the association, the film industry now recycles items from Hollywood sets, including wood and plastics.

The industry also uses energy-efficient lighting on sets and in production offices, uses biodiesel for power, has recycled paper on its sets and in crew offices, and transports cast and crew in hybrid vehicles. Ed is also a member of the Santa Monica Mountains Conservancy, the Coalition for Clean Air, Tree People, and the Natural Resources Defense Council, among many other groups dedicated to environmental conservation.

## Reservations about Ed's Activism

Though Ed got many acting jobs in the 1990s, his manager and agent did make him aware that there were people who were hesitant about hiring him. Some feared that his fiercely held stands on environmental conservation might cause a problem on the set. Ed wasn't interested in causing problems. He never felt that forcing his beliefs on others was the way to go.

In one instance, people on the set were worried that Ed would be upset because the recycling bins they had ordered hadn't arrived yet. Ed was happy

**Be Earth-Friendly: Recycle**

Recycle (below) whenever possible. Buy recycled products. Try not to waste things like paper, cardboard, string, and tape, so less will have to be made—and when less is produced, fewer greenhouse gases are released into the atmosphere.

about the recycling bins, but he hadn't asked for them or mentioned them, and he wasn't planning to. He appreciates whatever people try to do to help, but causing a major uproar over it is not his style.

## Making It Official

In August 2000, Ed married his long-time girlfriend, Rachelle Carson. In the process, he got some full-time help with his environmental projects, and a co-star in his own reality series. Rachelle and Ed were now officially the greenest couple in Tinseltown.

◀ This handsome fellow from Britain is the WEEE (Waste, Electrical and Electronic Equipment) man. Designed by London-based designer Paul Bonomini, the WEEE man is made out of about three tons of electrical and electronic waste, including five refrigerators, four lawnmowers, microwave ovens, TVs, vacuum cleaners, cell phones, and even computer mice. It stands 23 feet (seven m) tall. This sculpture represents the amount of electrical and electronic waste the average person will dispose of in a lifetime.

# Chapter 5
# Keeping Up with Ed

▲ Ed Begley, Jr. is pictured on an IZIP stationary bicycle during Project Greenhouse in Park City, Utah, in 2007. Ed is sipping an organic health beverage as he pedals.

Ed Begley, Jr. does have a computer, and he uses it every day. He also has many other modern conveniences in his home. To Ed, living green doesn't mean living in the Dark Ages; it simply means doing things with conscious attention to the environmental impact of our actions.

Take Ed's exercise bike, for instance. While many exercise bikes are plugged into the wall, drawing power, Ed's is generating power. Ed rewired the bike and has it tied into a battery bank that provides power to his house. Riding the bike 15 minutes a day helps recharge the battery bank, producing enough energy to keep his computer working all day without drawing any power from the power-company grid. This is just one of the ideas that Ed is asked about since becoming one of Hollywood's leading green spokespeople.

### Green Gardening

Another one of Ed's interests that has caught the attention of fellow Hollywood green-living converts is his passion for gardening. Ed has loved gardening since he was a child, and now he actually grows about 25 percent of what his family eats right on his own property.

By growing his own food, Ed knows the food is fresh. It's organic because he grows it that way, and he gets good exercise in the garden. He uses collected rainwater to water his plants, cutting down on the amount of water that comes out of the pipes to maintain the garden. Many movie and TV stars are now turning to gardening as a hobby, and as a way to eat and be healthy. Fruit and vegetable gardens are becoming more and more a part of the Hollywood landscape.

## Professional Success, Too

Hollywood big shots who once made light of Ed's green efforts have become some of his biggest supporters. Ed is busier than ever onstage and onscreen, big and small. Since the year 2000, Ed has appeared on an impressive list of TV shows, and he has had recurring roles on most of them. *Providence*, *7th Heaven*, *Jack & Bobby*, *Arrested Development*, *Kingdom Hospital*, *Six Feet Under*, *Boston Legal*, and *Veronica Mars* have all featured Ed. He also directed several episodes of NYPD Blue.

In 2003, Ed produced and directed a play he wrote, called *César and Ruben*. The play is a

### More Than One Cause

In addition to working to preserve the environment, Ed supports a variety of other causes as well, such as animal welfare. Ed has pets of his own, but he also cares for stray cats that have gathered at his home.

It started in the early 1990s, when a cat showed up at his back door. The cat wouldn't let Ed touch her, just feed her. After years of the cat having litters, which Ed dutifully had neutered and then put up for adoption, Ed caught her in a Have-A-Heart trap and brought her to the vet to be spayed.

Now that the drama has ended, the mom and several of her older offspring, ones for whom Ed was unable to find homes, live on Ed's roof. There is a space between each of the solar panels on the roof, and that's where the cats call home. There they enjoy shade from the Sun in summer and warmth from the Sun in the winter.

Ed is more than happy to feed the brood and provide for their needs for the rest of their days. The cats are very clean. They come down from the roof to eat and go to the "bathroom," and then it's back on the roof, where they savor the high life.

◀ These lucky cats were rescued as strays and given a home. Ed feels that the best thing animal lovers can do is to neuter or spay their pets to control animal overpopulation.

musical about United Farm Workers leader César Chávez and journalist Ruben Salazar. Chávez is one of Ed's idols. Rachelle Carson, Ed's wife, had a major role in the play, which received favorable reviews during its run in North Hollywood.

Another acting project close to Ed's heart was the 2008 HBO movie *Recount*, a film about the 2000 presidential election, which pitted George W. Bush against Al Gore, and its aftermath. Ed played David Boies, the attorney who represented Vice President Al Gore when the famous election case, Bush v. Gore, came before the United States Supreme Court.

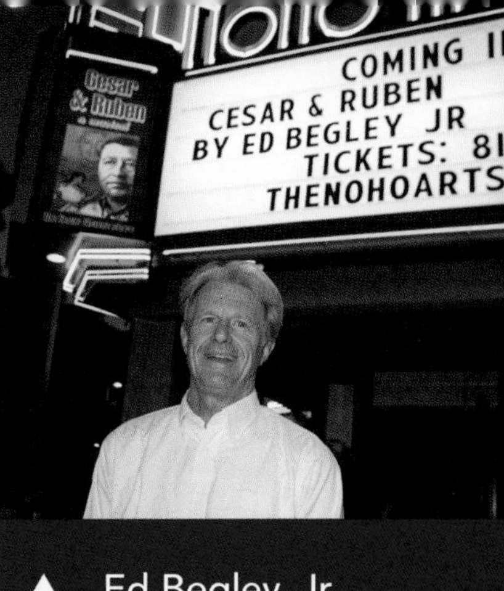


▲ Ed Begley, Jr. stands under the marquee on opening night, August 10, 2007, in North Hollywood for the play *César and Ruben*. Ed wrote and directed the play.

▼ Actress and environmental activist Daryl Hannah joins Ed to kick off Keep America Beautiful, a program that puts volunteers to work cleaning up litter and debris in over 15,000 communities across the United States.

## An Eco-Friendly Soapbox

With Ed's star on the rise, more people inside and outside the showbiz community were striking up conversations with him about the work he was doing to save the environment and his eco-friendly lifestyle. "I do feel lucky to have this opportunity to have the soapbox, to have the microphone, to have the megaphone for a moment to talk," Ed said. "I think we have to use that moment when it arises. But there's a great responsibility that comes with that…you want to have your facts right." So Ed has done a great deal of research on the environment.

He has read published papers on the subject, making sure the information he was getting and giving to other people was factual and validated. "More than half the living Nobel Laureates have told me about some of the very real problems. Not anecdotal stuff, not baloney; it's stuff from peer-reviewed studies," Ed pointed out.

People have come to trust Ed and the information and advice he gives about the environment because his information is so solid and reliable. Ed speaks about environmental issues at colleges and civic meetings and gives many interviews on TV and in magazines, urging people to do whatever they can to help reduce the size of their carbon footprint.

Ed has also offered an array of tips on living green on his TV show, *Living with Ed*. While Ed and Rachelle presented a lot of good information on the show, Ed felt it was TV—the tool he used to give out that information—that resonated with so many viewers.

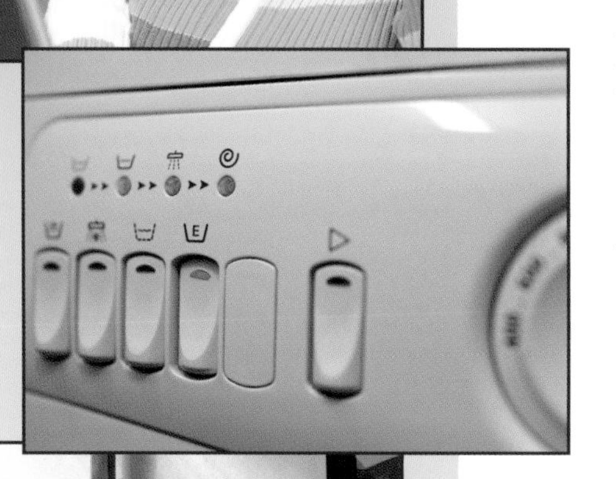

## The Power of Comedy

That tool was comedy. Ed knows comedy can be very powerful. *Living with Ed* was funny, which made it enjoyable and drew people to Ed and his message. Viewers wanted to see what would happen next, what Ed's next project would be, and what Rachelle's reaction to it would be. In the process, the show was giving people some pretty good ideas about how to save the planet.

▲ Three ways to save energy (top to bottom): Wear a sweater instead of turning up the thermostat; choose the energy-saving option on appliances; collect rainwater to use in watering plants in the garden.

Ed always says that he is still just a working actor, not a millionaire. He lives on a budget and understands that most other people do too, so he urges people to do whatever they can, and whatever fits into their budget.

"You take a small step and you prove to yourself that you can do it. You compare your electric bills and see that the change you made was good for your wallet. You see how much money you saved and you see how little it affected the quality of your life. I'll bet you barely even noticed the difference," Ed said.

"When you feel more confident and more comfortable —better acclimated, if you will—make one or two more changes, and so on and so on."

Ed feels this is a formula for success that anybody can follow.

## His Own Product Line

Ed always gets questions about which cleaning fluids are safe to use for the environment. With that in mind, he launched a line of cleaning products several years ago called Begley's Best. That's the project his daughter Amanda is working with him on.

Ed wants to develop Begley's Best into the same type of project as the late Paul Newman's food products marketed under the Newman's Own brand. Like the money made with Newman's Own, proceeds from Begley's Best go to charity

**Recycling Out of Love**

Here's one way to show your love for trees. For every four-foot (1.2-m) pile of newspaper that is recycled, a tree is saved. If everyone in the United States recycled just one newspaper a week, it could save 36 million trees a year!

That's not the only reason to recycle newspaper and other types of paper. Recycling also saves space in landfills, and the production of recycled paper uses less water and less energy, and causes less air pollution, than making paper from scratch.

How much water is saved by making paper from recycled materials versus new materials? Close to 80 percent!

▼ Save a tree, and eventually a whole forest, by recycling newspapers. Newsprint comes from wood pulp, which is derived from trees. Recycling even one newspaper a day can make a difference.

▲ Everyone can make simple changes to help the environment, such as riding a bicycle instead of taking a car.

▼ With his wife Rachelle and daughter Hayden, Ed attended the screening party to launch *Living with Ed* in December 2006. The entire family appears in the eco-friendly reality TV series.

as well—in Ed's case, environmental causes. Ed's all-purpose cleaner is made from all-natural, nontoxic, and totally biodegradable ingredients. It's the cleaner he has used for years around his house. The ingredients include extracts from olive seeds, pine, corn, de-acidified citrus, and fermented sugarcane roots.

The all-purpose cleaner is made strong enough to dissolve grease and grime without harming surfaces made of plastic, wood, leather, tile, chrome, linoleum, and stainless steel. The product line also includes a spot remover, and the products are completely eco-friendly. Ed said people don't necessarily have the time to make a cleaning product like this themselves. Part of helping save the planet is making the task as easy for people as possible.

**Making Progress**

Does environmental activism work? Ed definitely thinks so! Today there is 50 percent less air pollution in Los Angeles than in 1970, even though there are more cars on the road. People cared about the environment, forced elected officials in California to take action to clean up the smog, and cut down on air pollution.

There is no doubt that Ed Begley, Jr. has raised the eco-friendly bar pretty high, but he doesn't expect everyone to reach for that bar. He would just like to see everyone do something: "Anyone who takes a step toward helping the environment makes me happy."

# Chronology

| | |
|---|---|
| **1949** | Edward James Begley, Jr. is born on September 16, in Los Angeles |
| **1962** | Ed's father, Ed Begley, Sr. wins an Academy Award for Best Supporting Actor for his role in *Sweet Bird of Youth* |
| **1967** | Ed graduates from Van Nuys High School. Begins theater and cinematography classes at Los Angeles Valley College. Lands his first TV sitcom role on *My Three Sons* |
| **1969** | Makes his film debut in an uncredited role in the Disney film *The Computer Wore Tennis Shoes* |
| **1970** | Participates in the first Earth Day observance and becomes a committed environmentalist. Buys his first electric car |
| **1973** | Gets a starring role in the short-lived TV series *Roll Out* |
| **1976** | Lands his first recurring role on the sitcom *Mary Hartman, Mary Hartman*. Marries Ingrid Taylor, in October |
| **1977** | Daughter, Amanda, is born on October 3 |
| **1978** | Appears as Ensign Greenbean on *Battlestar Galactica* |
| **1979** | Son, Nicholas, is born on January 4 |
| **1982** | Gets the role of Dr. Victor Ehrlich on the medical drama *St. Elsewhere* |
| **1982–1988** | Plays Dr. Victor Ehrlich on *St. Elsewhere* for the show's entire six-year run |
| **1983** | Is nominated for his first Emmy Award for his work on *St. Elsewhere*. (During the show's six-year run, he was nominated for an Emmy a total of six times) |
| **1984** | Appears in the movie *This Is Spinal Tap*, directed by Rob Reiner |
| **1987** | Is nominated for a Golden Globe Award for Best Supporting Actor in a TV series for his role on *St. Elsewhere* |
| **1989** | Ed and his wife, Ingrid, are divorced in October. Wins a role opposite Meryl Streep in the film *She-Devil* |
| **1990** | Buys a two-bedroom home in the San Fernando Valley, which later becomes the setting for his reality TV show, *Living with Ed*, on eco-friendly living |
| **1991** | Appears with Stockard Channing in *Meet the Applegates* |

| | |
|---|---|
| **1992** | Becomes a full-fledged vegetarian. Does character voices for the popular animated *Batman* TV series |
| **1993** | Meets Rachelle Carson at an environmental event |
| **1994** | Appears with Danny DeVito in the film *Renaissance Man*, directed by Penny Marshall |
| **1995** | Has a role in the film *Batman Forever* |
| **1998** | Appears in an episode of hit TV show *The West Wing* |
| **2000** | Becomes a member of the Board of Governors of the Academy of Motion Picture Arts and Sciences (Actors Branch). Marries Rachelle Carson in August. Appears in *Homicide: The Movie* |
| **2001–2003** | Has a recurring role in the TV drama *7th Heaven* |
| **2003** | Produces and directs *César and Ruben*, a play he wrote. Makes his TV directing debut at the helm of the drama *NYPD Blue* |
| **2004–2005** | Has a recurring role on the TV drama *Jack & Bobby* |
| **2005–2006** | Has a recurring role on the TV sitcom *Arrested Development* |
| **2006–2007** | Has a recurring role on the TV drama *Veronica Mars* |
| **2007** | The eco-friendly-living, reality TV show, *Living with Ed*, debuts on HGTV, in January. The Academy Awards and events relating to it go green. Ed launches his line of eco-friendly cleaning products, Begley's Best |
| **2008** | Ed's book, *Living Like Ed*, is published. Ed appears in the HBO movie *Recount*, the story of the disputed 2000 presidential election |

# Glossary

**acclimated** Used to; feeling comfortable with

**amenities** Conveniences; luxuries

**character actor** An actor who generally plays non-starring, supporting roles

**cinematography** Camerawork in the movies

**curb** To stop; to put an end to

**dark comedy** Comedy that pokes fun at a serious, or even dreadful, situation

**ensemble** A group that is working together as a whole, as in a collection of actors who come to be identified with a single show

**fossil fuel** Fuels, such as oil or coal, made from the decaying remains of plants and animals that lived millions of years ago

**global warming** The warming of Earth's air and oceans as a result of a buildup of heat-trapping gases, called greenhouse gases, in the atmosphere

**greenhouse gas** A gas, such as carbon dioxide, that helps warm the planet by keeping heat in the atmosphere; too many greenhouse gases trapped in the atmosphere by pollution can lead to global warming

**grid** A distribution network; a way of sending power, such as electricity, to individual homes and businesses

**hybrid cars** Cars that use two or more distinct power sources, such as gasoline and electricity

**ironically** Relating to a situation that is completely unexpected and goes against conventional wisdom, often with amusing or surprising results

**knack** Ability

**landfill** Large areas that serve as dumping grounds for trash; the trash and other waste is then covered with dirt and trees and grass are planted

**madcap antics** Crazy, out-of-control, completely unexpected behavior

**organic** Grown without using artificial fertilizer or pesticides

**parody** A takeoff; something that makes fun of something else

**piqued** Intrigued; aroused interest or curiosity in

**pollute** To release harmful substances into the air, water, or land

**prototype** Sample; model

**proximity** Closeness; nearness

**resonated** Struck a chord; seemed appropriate

**rotund** Large and round

**smog** A mix of smoke and fog in the air; a form of pollution

**sustainable** Able to meet present needs without causing future damage or depletion of resources, such as food or water

**vantage point** Point of view

**zany** Funny, wacky

# Further Information

## Books

Begley, Ed., Jr. *Living Like Ed: A Guide to the Eco-Friendly Life*. Clarkson Potter/Publishers, 2008.

Cone, Marla. *Silent Snow: The Slow Poisoning of the Arctic*. Grove Press, 2005.

Gore, Al. *An Inconvenient Truth: The Planetary Emergency of Global Warming and What We Can Do About It*. Rodale Books, 2006.

McNamee, Gregory. *Careers in Renewable Energy: Get a Green Energy Job*. American Solar Energy Society, 2008.

## Web sites

*www.edbegley.com*
The official Web site of Ed Begley, Jr. contains a great deal of information about saving the environment, and even allows visitors to ask Ed questions.

*www.solarenergy.org*
The Web site of Solar Energy International (SEI) has information on what countries all over the world—even developing nations—are doing to try to harness and use solar energy. Includes updates on new solar technology and breaking solar energy news as well.

*www.ases.org*
This is the site of the American Solar Energy Society, which focuses on the latest advancements in solar energy and how they can be used in everyday living.

*www.sierraclub.org*
The Web site of America's oldest and largest environmental organization, the Sierra Club, contains information on all aspects of saving the environment, as well as the latest projects and efforts to save Earth and how everyone can get involved.

*www.climatecrisiscoalition.org*
The official Web site of the Climate Crisis Coalition, this site deals with the urgent matter of climate change and what can be done about it.

*www.panda.org*
A site sponsored by the World Wildlife Fund that is dedicated to conservation and the latest developments in the field. It contains news items, especially focusing on how conservation-related issues impact the animal world.

# Index

**About the Author**

Robert Grayson is an award-winning former newspaper reporter and author of young adult biographies. Robert's stories on arts and entertainment, sports, and pets have appeared in many publications. Among his articles are celebrity interviews with TV and movie stars.



Printed in the U.S.A. — CG